SPECIAL
CEREMONIES
Births

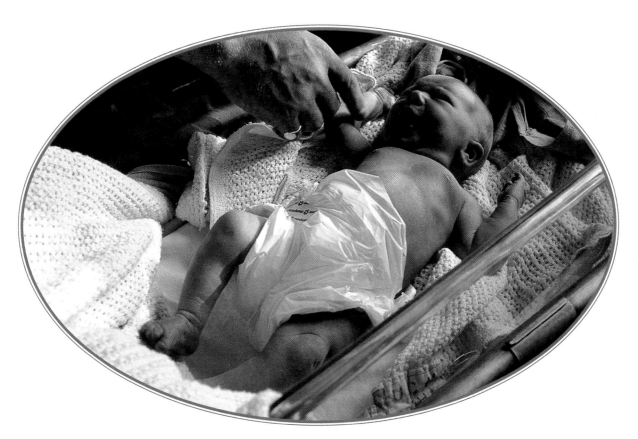

Polly Goodman

WAYLAND

SPECIAL
CEREMONIES
Births

This differentiated text version is by Polly Goodman, first published in Great Britain in 2005 by Wayland, an imprint of Hachette Children's Books.

This paperback edition published in 2006 by Wayland, an imprint of Hachette Children's Books.

Original designer: Tim Mayer
Layout for this edition: Jane Hawkins

Consultants:
Rasamandala Das;
Working Group on Sikhs and Education (WORKSE);
Jane Clements, The Council of Christians and Jews;
Jonathan Gorsky, The Council of Christians and Jews;
Dr Fatma Amer, The London Central Mosque;
The Clear Vision Trust.

Picture acknowledgements: Circa Picture Library 15 (John Smith), 16, 18, 22, 28, 29; Hutchison Library 4 (Juliet Highet), 9 (N Durrell McKenna), 24 (Liba Taylor); Panos Pictures 6 (Betty Press), 8 (Jon Spaull), 17 (Giacomo Airozzi), 19 (Chris Stowers), 21 (Jean-Leo Dugast), 27 (Jimmy Holmes); Peter Sanders 14; Tony Stone Images 1, 5; Trip 7 (A Tovy), 10 (I Genut), 11 (I Brahim), 12, 13 (I Genut), 20 (H Rogers), 23, 25 (F Good), 26 (B Dhanjal).

British Library Cataloguing in Publication Data
Goodman, Polly
Births. - Differentiated ed. - (Special Ceremonies)
1. Birth customs - Religious aspects - Juvenile literature
I. Title II. Dineen, Jacqueline
203.8'1

ISBN-10: 0 7502 4972 2
ISBN-13: 978 0 7502 4972 0

Printed in China

Wayland
Hachette Children's Books
338 Euston Road, London NW1 3BH

Contents

Getting Ready

The birth of a new baby is a very special time. As they wait for the baby's arrival, parents think about how they will bring up their child. Many parents will want to share their religion with their children. Religion can help parents to guide their children in their everyday lives.

In the months before the birth, many parents worry about the health of their baby. When the baby is born safely, it is time to celebrate and give thanks.

As the time for the birth gets nearer, parents think of a name for their child. ▶

People from different religions welcome a new baby in different ways. But whatever their religion, most people celebrate the birth of a new baby with a special ceremony, when they give the baby its name.

Family members visit the mother and her new-born baby to wish them luck and happiness. ▼

THE BABY'S ROOM

A new baby will need a cot to sleep in and clothes to wear. Before the birth, the parents prepare the baby's room. When the baby is born, friends help by giving presents of clothes and toys.

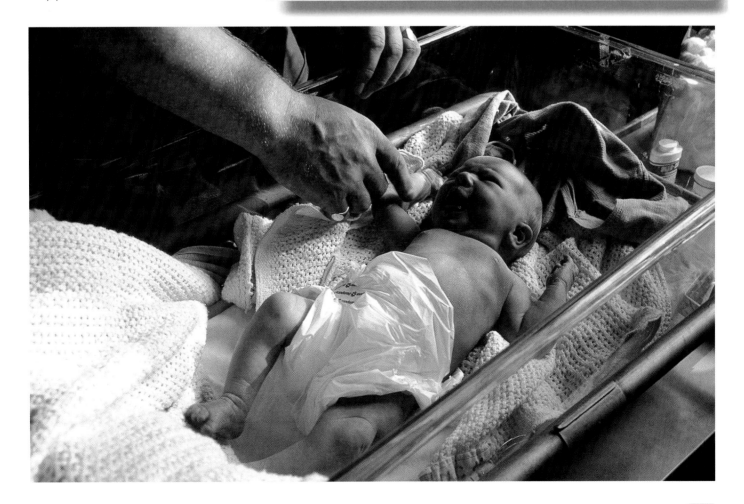

The Christian Tradition

◄ This nativity scene shows the baby Jesus, with his parents, Mary and Joseph.

The most important birth celebration for Christians is the birth of Jesus Christ. Christians believe that Jesus was born just over 2,000 years ago, in a stable in the town of Bethlehem. Most Christians celebrate his birth on 25 December, which is Christmas Day.

Christians usually go to church over Christmas and decorate their homes with Christmas trees, holly and mistletoe. They often have a nativity scene, which is a model of the scene in the stable, where Jesus Christ was born.

▲ Some couples go to the house of the Virgin Mary, in Greece, to pray for a child.

HOLY BOOK

'And God blessed them, and God said unto them, Be fruitful, and multiply, and replenish the earth, and subdue it...'

From *The Bible*, *Genesis* 1: 28

Having children is important to many Christians. The Christian holy book, the *Bible*, mentions the importance of family life many times.

Sometimes a pregnant woman asks a priest to give a prayer for her baby to be born safely. The priest may visit the mother at home or in hospital. He uses special oil to make the sign of the cross on the mother's forehead. The cross is the symbol of Christianity.

▲ In this baptism ceremony, the priest pours holy water over the baby's head.

Baptism

Christian parents often celebrate the birth of their baby in a baptism ceremony. Another name for this ceremony is a christening, because this is also the time that children are given their Christian names. Most Christian parents baptize or christen their children when they are just a few months old.

Before the baptism or christening, the parents choose two or three godparents. These close friends or relatives are given a special duty to take care of the child if the parents become unable to. Godparents also give support and guidance to their godchild as he or she grows up.

LYNDA'S STORY

'My name is Lynda. Yesterday I went to the christening of my baby brother, Mark. He wore a long white dress that my grandmother made. After the ceremony, we walked to the front of the church in a procession. The vicar held Mark up in the air for everyone to see. Then he gave him back to my mum.'

The ceremony

Baptisms or christenings usually take place in a morning church service. The parents and godparents stand with the baby at the font. They make promises to help the child grow up in the Christian faith. Then the baby is given its Christian name.

The priest or minister pours a little holy water over the baby's forehead and makes the sign of the cross. The water is a symbol for washing away the child's sins and starting a new life with God. The family is given a candle and the priest welcomes the baby into the Christian church.

After the ceremony, friends and relatives often have a party at the parents' home. They give the baby presents. Silver gifts are supposed to bring good luck.

Parents ask people they trust to become godparents to their children. It is a great honour to become a godparent. ▼

The Jewish Tradition

The most important ceremony for Jewish baby boys is circumcision. In the *Torah*, the Jewish holy book, it is recorded that God said, 'Every male among you who is eight days old must be circumcised.' God said this to Abraham, who founded the Jewish nation about 2,300 years ago.

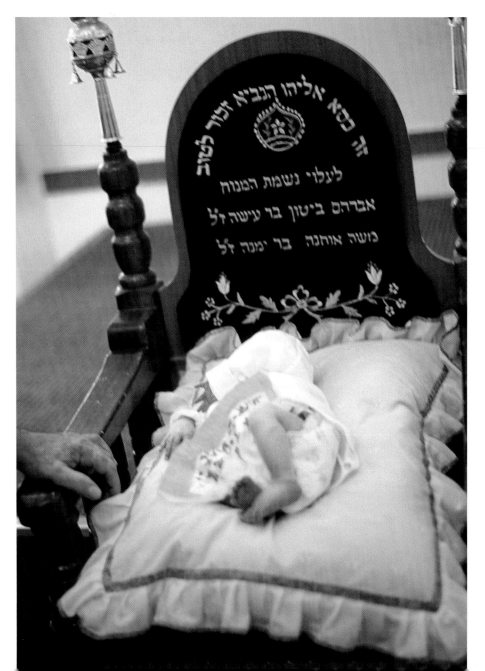

◄ This baby is lying on Elijah's chair. Elijah was a prophet who Jews believe protects children.

HOLY BOOK

'This is My covenant, which ye shall keep between Me and you and thy seed after thee: every male among you shall be circumcised.

And ye shall be circumcised in the flesh of your foreskin; and it shall be a token of a covenant between Me and you.

And he that is eight days old shall be circumcised among you, every male throughout your generations...'

From *Genesis 17*, the first book of the *Bible*.

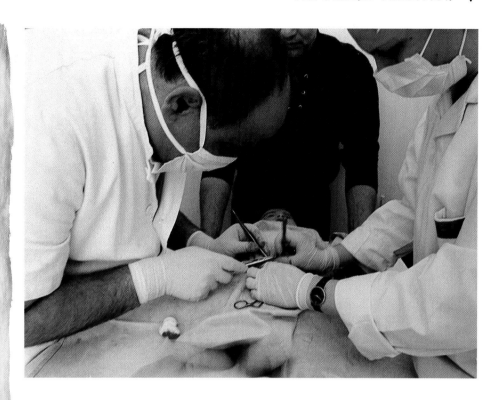

▲ When a baby boy is circumcised, his foreskin is removed.

What is circumcision?

Circumcision is a simple operation, which can help to prevent disease. It usually takes place when a baby boy is eight days old. A specially trained person, called a *mohel*, removes the foreskin of the baby's penis. The mohel is usually a Jewish doctor.

The circumcision often takes place in the boy's home, but sometimes it takes place in the synagogue. The ceremony is a sign of a boy's entrance into the Jewish faith.

▲ In the synagogue, the godfather carries the baby to the rabbi, the leader of the synagogue.

The circumcision ceremony

At the beginning of the circumcision ceremony everyone welcomes the baby boy, saying: 'Blessed be he that cometh.' After the baby is circumcised there is a prayer called a *kiddush*, when everyone drinks wine. The baby is given a sip of wine from a cup that is blessed.

Today, some Jewish people have a ceremony for baby girls. There is no operation, but people welcome the baby girl into the Jewish community. They say, 'Blessed is she that cometh.'

RUDI'S STORY

'My name is Rudi. My brother was circumcised last week. The *mohel* reminded us about a part in the *Torah*. It says that circumcision is a reminder of our promise to worship only God. The *mohel* said a blessing while he did the circumcision. At the end of the ceremony, we had a party to celebrate.

Naming ceremony

After the circumcision ceremony, the baby is given its name. Jewish parents often choose the name of a member of the family, or someone in Jewish history.

If the circumcision took place at home, the parents take their baby to synagogue for the naming ceremony. The people in the synagogue welcome the baby to the Jewish faith. Boys and girls can be named in a joint ceremony.

After the ceremonies, family and friends celebrate with a special meal and give the child presents.

At the celebration dinner, family and friends make speeches about growing up. ▼

The Muslim Tradition

Muslims say that a baby is a gift from Allah (the Muslim word for God). It is a very happy occasion. The first words that a new-born baby should hear is the call to prayer. This is a special prayer, called the *adhan*, which calls all Muslims to the mosque to pray.

The *adhan* is whispered in the baby's right ear. Then another prayer, called the *iqamah*, is whispered in the baby's left ear. By hearing these prayers as soon as he or she is born, the baby starts life as a Muslim from the very beginning.

◀ Muslim children learn to say prayers when they are very young.

Sweetness

In another ceremony, called the *tahnik*, a piece of sugar, honey or date is rubbed on to the baby's gums. In Muslim tradition this makes the baby sweet-tempered and is a symbol of a happy life.

HOLY BOOK

To God belongs the dominion
Of the heavens and the earth.
He creates what he wills
(And plans). He bestows
(Children) male or female
According to his Will (and Plan).

From *The Qur'an, Sura XLII: 49*

Muslims pray five times a day. Many go to the mosque on fridays for the midday prayers. ▶

▲ Many Muslim babies have their heads shaved before their naming ceremony.

Naming ceremony

When the baby is about seven days old, the family holds a naming ceremony, called the *aqiqah*. Many parents shave their baby's head to symbolise the beginning of a new life. It is Muslim tradition to give the same weight as the baby's hair in gold or silver to the poor. Parents usually give more than just the weight of the hair to show thanks for the birth.

After prayers are said, the baby is given its name. Then family and friends have a celebration dinner.

IMRAN'S STORY

'My name is Imran. My baby sister Layla was born last week. We invited our friends and family round to our house for a special ceremony. Everyone was really excited to see Layla. After washing, we said some prayers. Then Mum gave Layla a bit of honey and Dad made a speech. He told everyone Layla's name. Then we went for a big meal in the restaurant nearby.'

Circumcision

Like Jewish boys, Muslim boys are also circumcised. If the baby is healthy, he is often circumcised at the same time as his naming ceremony. If he is not well, the ceremony is left for a few months. In some countries, Muslim boys are not circumcised until they are over four years old.

Muslim children are often named after family members, or members of the Prophet Muhammad's ﷺ family. ▼

The Buddhist Tradition

▲ This painting shows the Buddha's mother dreaming of a white elephant before the Buddha was born.

An important birth celebration for Buddhists is the birth of the Buddha, the founder of Buddhism. This is often celebrated at *Wesak*, on the day of the full moon in May or June.

At *Wesak*, many Buddhists visit their temple and place flowers, incense and candles in front of statues of the Buddha. They listen to the teachings of the Buddha and chant verses from the scriptures. Some people decorate their homes with lanterns and there may be processions through the streets.

SACRED WRITINGS

May all without exception be happy:
Beings seen or unseen,
Those who live near or far away,
Those who are born
And those who are not yet born.
May all beings be happy.

From the *Metta Sutta*
(the Buddha's words on kindness)

Stories of the Buddha's birth

The Buddha was born over 2,500 years ago. Buddhist parents tell their babies stories about his birth, and try to be wise and kind like him.

One story tells how, before the Buddha was born, his mother dreamed about a white elephant. People saw this as a sign. It meant that her child would be a teacher who would guide the world. Another story tells how the Buddha stood up and walked, straight after he was born. This may not be true but it symbolizes how special the Buddha was.

In the temple, Buddhists listen to the Buddha's teachings and chant Buddhist texts. ▼

Blessing the baby

Many Buddhist parents have their baby blessed when it is born. They take the baby to the monastery or temple, or ask monks or nuns to come to their home.

The monks and nuns wear long robes. They chant blessings for health and happiness. Chanting makes their mind focus on what they are saying.

This monk flicks holy water over a baby at a blessing. The baby's brother is joining the prayers. ▼

▲ Buddhists place flowers in front of statues of the Buddha to show their love for him.

JOANNE'S STORY

'My name is Joanne. My baby brother was blessed last week. We invited monks to our house. They chanted verses and said many blessings. I asked them why Buddhists meditate. They said it was to free your mind so you can understand more about life.'

Naming ceremony

When they are about a month old, many Buddhist babies have a naming ceremony. In the temple or monastery, their parents kneel in front of a statue of the Buddha and give flowers, candles and incense. They choose a special name with a beautiful meaning for their child. Family and friends come to welcome the child.

The Hindu Tradition

As with other religions, family life is very important to Hindus. Most couples get married in order to have children. Visits to the *mandir* or temple, the Hindu place of worship, are also very important.

When a woman becomes pregnant, members of her family go to the temple to pray for the child's health and happiness. Afterwards there is a feast for the family members.

The mother-to-be reads prayers from Hindu scriptures to the baby in her womb. She hopes the scriptures will protect her child. Reading also helps the mother to feel close to her baby.

When a Hindu mother reads prayers to her baby in the womb, it starts the baby's religious life. ▶

Steps of life

Hindus believe there are sixteen steps in a person's life, and each step should be celebrated with a special ritual. The rituals are called *samskaras*. The first three *samskaras* take place before a child is born. The next six *samskaras* take place in the child's first few years. The last step takes place after a person has died.

On the day a baby is born, a priest visits the family. He works out the position of the stars and planets at the time of the baby's birth. This is called a horoscope. The horoscope is used to work out the baby's future.

◄ Fortune-tellers predict the future for babies using the time and day they were born.

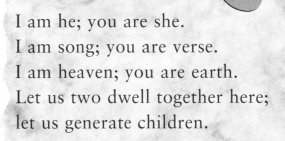

HOLY BOOK 🕉

I am he; you are she.
I am song; you are verse.
I am heaven; you are earth.
Let us two dwell together here;
let us generate children.

From *Atharva Veda: Marriage Mantra*

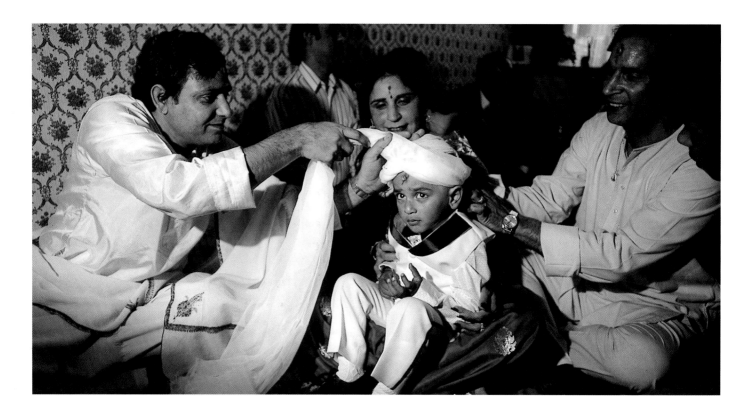

▲ This boy is about to have his head shaved to remove any evil from past lives.

A prayer for wisdom

Another ceremony takes place on the day a child is born. In front of a Hindu priest, the father dips a gold ring in honey and holds it to the baby's mouth. The father and priest say, 'May your life be as precious as gold.' Then the father or priest whispers a prayer for wisdom in the baby's ear.

DEVA'S STORY

'My name is Deva. When my baby sister was born, we asked the priest about the names we could call her. We held a naming ceremony, on the twelfth day after she was born. After the ceremony we ate some special food that was blessed, called *prasadam*.'

The first haircut

When a baby is around one year old, its hair is cut for the first time. Hindus believe that people have many lives, which means that each baby has many past lives. By shaving the baby's hair, parents make sure they remove any evil from the past and give the child a fresh start. Some children are three or five years old before they have their first haircut.

Parents keep the hair from their child's first haircut to remember this important event. ▼

The Sikh Tradition

▲ Sikhs carry the Sikh flag through the streets to celebrate the birth of Guru Nanak.

The most important birth celebration for Sikhs is the birth of Guru Nanak, the founder of Sikhism. Everyone goes to the *gurdwara* or temple, the Sikh place of worship. People read prayers from the Sikh holy book, the *Guru Granth Sahib*. They read the whole book from start to finish without stopping.

Welcoming the baby

Sikh parents teach their children the Sikh way of life. This father and son are in front of the Golden Temple in India. It is the holiest place for Sikhs. ▼

Sikhs believe that a new baby is a gift from God. When a baby is born, the parents tell all their friends and relatives the good news. They give sweets to friends and neighbours to show their joy.

Sometimes a member of the Sikh community visits the home and gives the baby a few drops of honey and water. He may read a special verse from the *Guru Granth Sahib*. It was written by a Guru on the birth of his son.

HOLY BOOK

'The True Lord has sent the child. The long lived child has been born by good fortune. The Sikhs sing God's praises in their joy.'

From the *Guru Granth Sahib*, page 396.

Naming ceremony

Soon after the birth, a Sikh baby has a naming
ceremony. This usually takes place at the *gurdwara*.
The parents read hymns of thanksgiving from the
Guru Granth Sahib. The family prepare a sacred
pudding called *Karah Parshad* for everyone to share.

▲ At a naming
ceremony, sweet water,
called *Amrit*, is given to
the mother and baby.

HARDEEP'S STORY

'My name is Hardeep. My baby brother had his naming ceremony last week. At the end of the service the *granthi* (the person who does the readings) gave him a steel bracelet called a *kara*. The round shape of the bracelet stands for the truth of God without a beginning or end. The steel stands for strength.'

Choosing a name

During the naming ceremony, the *Guru Granth Sahib* is placed on a platform. The parents bring a new cover for it. Everyone says a prayer that mentions the parents' names.

After the prayer, the *Guru Granth Sahib* is opened at random. The parents listen for the prayer that appears when the book is opened. Then they choose a name for their child that begins with the first letter of the prayer. Girls' names are followed by *'Kaur'*, which means princess. Boys' names are followed by *'Singh'*, which means lion. Sometimes a family name is added, too.

Sikhs stand before the *Guru Granth Sahib* on the platform on the right. ▼

Glossary

Allah the Muslim word for God.

Bible the Christian and Jewish scriptures.

Buddha an Indian prince called Siddhartha Gautama, who founded Buddhism.

covenant an agreement entered into between God and a person or people.

faith another word for religion, or a belief in a religion.

font a basin containing holy water.

granthi a reader of the *Guru Granth Sahib*.

guru a Sikh leader.

Guru Granth Sahib the Sikh holy book.

horoscope a map of the stars and planets made at the time of a person's birth, used to predict the future.

incense a scented stick that is burned to give a fragrant smell.

kara a steel bracelet worn by Sikh men and women.

mandir a Hindu temple or place of worship.

meditate to sit peacefully and calm the mind.

mohel an official in Judaism.

monastery a place where monks live and worship.

mosque a Muslim place of worship.

prophet a person who brings a message from God or Allah.

Qur'an the Muslim holy book.

rabbi a teacher of the Jewish religion.

ritual an activity that is part of a ceremony.

scriptures holy writings.

symbolize to represent something.

synagogue a Jewish place of worship.

Torah the Jewish holy writings, written over two scrolls.

Books to Read

Beliefs and Cultures series: *Buddhist; Christian; Hindu; Jewish; Muslim* (Watts, 2003)

My Life, My Religion series: *Anglican Curate; Catholic Priest; Hindu Priest; Jewish Rabbi; Muslim Imam; Sikh Granthi* (Watts, 2001)

Our Culture series: *Buddhist; Hindu; Jewish; Muslim; Sikh* (Watts, 2003)

Places of Worship series: *Buddhist Temples; Catholic Churches; Hindu Temples; Mosques; Protestant Churches; Sikh Gurdwaras; Synagogues* (Heinemann, 2000)

Rites of Passage: Naming Ceremonies by Mandy Ross (Heinemann, 2004)

What's Special to Me?: Religious Buildings; Religious Food by Anita Ganeri (Hodder Wayland, 2000)

What I Believe by Alan Brown and Andrew Langley (Hodder Wayland, 2000)

A World of Festivals: Life and Death by Jean Coppendale (Chrysalis, 2005)

A Year of Religious Festivals: My Buddhist Year; My Christian Year; My Hindu Year; My Jewish Year; My Muslim Year; My Sikh Year by Cath Senker (Hodder Wayland, 2004)

Index

All the numbers in **bold** refer to photographs